GERMS AND DISEASE

WHAT ARE VIRUSES?

By Kathryn Kroe

Cavendish Square
New York

Published in 2023 by Cavendish Square Publishing, LLC
29 East 21st Street, New York, NY 10010

Website: cavendishsq.com

Library of Congress Cataloging-in-Publication Data

Names: Kroe, Kathryn, author.
Title: What are viruses? / Kathryn Kroe.
Description: First. | New York : Cavendish Square Publishing, [2023] |
Series: Germs and disease | Includes index.
Identifiers: LCCN 2021056087 | ISBN 9781502665348 (library binding) | ISBN 9781502665331 (paperback) | ISBN 9781502665355 (ebook)
Subjects: LCSH: Viruses—Juvenile literature.
Classification: LCC QR365 .K76 2023 | DDC 579.2—dc23/eng/20211116
LC record available at https://lccn.loc.gov/2021056087

Editor: Kathryn Kroe
Copyeditor: Jane Katirgis
Designer: Andrea Davison-Bartolotta

The photographs in this book are used by permission and through the courtesy of: Cover martynowi.cz/Shutterstock.com; series art (backgrounds) CHIARI VFX/Shutterstock.com; p. 5 stockcreations/Shutterstock.com; p. 6 Tatiana Shepeleva/Shutterstock.com; p. 8 Freeograph/Shutterstock.com; p. 10 Di Studio/Shutterstock.com; p. 12 Freedomz/Shutterstock.com; p. 14 Studio Romantic/Shutterstock.com; p. 16 fotohay/Shutterstock.com; p. 18 Daisy Daisy/Shutterstock.com; p. 21 Ekaterina_Molchanova/Shutterstock.com; p. 23 Chinnapong/Shutterstock.com; p. 24 Halfpoint/Shutterstock.com; p. 26 Kateryna Kon/Shutterstock.com; p. 29 Schira/Shutterstock.com; p. 30 Aldona Griskeviciene/Shutterstock.com; p. 31 namtipStudio/Shutterstock.com; p. 32 Jose Gil/Shutterstock.com; p. 34 soul of pic/Shutterstock.com; p. 37 Gorlov-KV/Shutterstock.com; p. 38 BlueRingMedia/Shutterstock.com; p. 39 digidreamgrafix/Shutterstock.com; p. 40 (main) Fahroni/Shutterstock.com; p. 40 (red circle) Oakview Studios/Shutterstock.com.

CPSIA compliance information: Batch #CSCSQ23: For further information contact Cavendish Square Publishing LLC, New York, New York, at 1-877-980-4450.

Printed in the United States of America

CONTENTS

INTRODUCTION

Viruses have been a topic that has recently been impossible to ignore. In late 2019, a new virus in the coronavirus family was detected in China and began to spread rapidly. This variation would eventually be known as coronavirus disease 2019 (COVID-19) and would lead to the first **pandemic** many people around the world had ever lived through. We had seen other coronaviruses before in people and animals, many causing only mild symptoms such as those of a cold. We had even seen coronaviruses that were more dangerous, such as severe acute respiratory syndrome (SARS) and Middle Eastern respiratory syndrome (MERS). The nature of viruses and how easily they mutate still made COVID-19 an unfamiliar foe.

COVID-19 didn't start in the United States, but by January 2020, the first case had been confirmed in the state of Washington. By the end of 2021, there had been well over 280 million confirmed cases worldwide, with more than 5 million deaths. While our scientific and medical knowledge of the specific COVID-19 virus was limited to start, doctors continued to try to get ahead of this virus, and guidance on fighting it continued to be updated. Our knowledge of other coronaviruses and the nature of viruses in general have been invaluable to fighting the pandemic.

COVID-19 is one of the more devastating examples of this type of germ. Viruses are behind many types of illness, from mild colds to severe diseases such as acquired immunodeficiency syndrome (AIDS) caused by the human immunodeficiency virus (HIV). Even COVID-19 itself is mild for some and severe for others. Viruses have been found all over our planet. Researchers estimate that 380 trillion viruses live inside and on the human body, which is 10 times the number of bacteria. These tiny viruses, which are not even cells themselves, invade other organisms and are an unavoidable part of our lives.

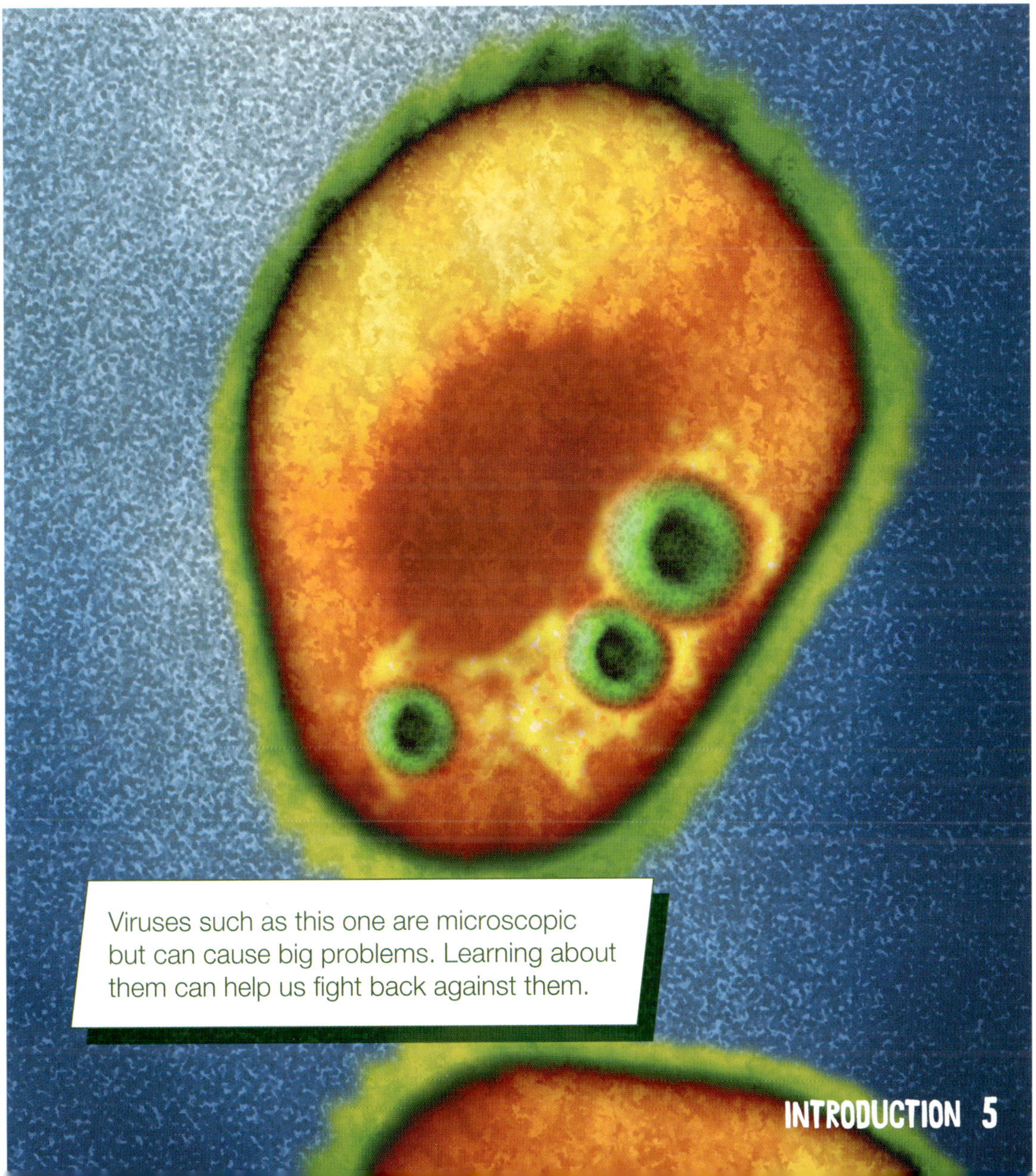

Viruses such as this one are microscopic but can cause big problems. Learning about them can help us fight back against them.

DNA is shaped like a double helix. It is the genetic material that makes up some viruses.

CHAPTER 1

HOW DO VIRUSES MAKE US SICK?

Viruses are even smaller than cells. In fact, these tiny bits of genetic material are so small they can even invade other microscopic organisms such as bacteria. They are made up of strands of **deoxyribonucleic acid** (DNA) or **ribonucleic acid** (RNA) surrounded by protein. Viruses need a living **host**, or cell, to reproduce. This means they cannot live long outside of a body, on surfaces, or in the air. This also means they are always looking for an opportunity to enter a body and invade its cells. If they are able to invade, they infect the host cell to replicate, often killing it and damaging the host.

Spreading Viruses

Some viruses spread through the air. Cold viruses are spread by coughing and sneezing. Other viruses spread through contaminated food or water, from mother to child in the womb or through breast milk, from biting insects, or from physical contact with infected people.

Cells are selective about which chemicals they let in or keep out. Special receptors on a cell's surface permit entry to only those chemicals the cell needs. A receptor is like a lock. The needed

Many viruses spread through surfaces and direct contact, but some viruses are capable of spreading from mother to baby even before the baby is born.

chemical is like the key that unlocks the receptor. Once a virus is spread, it mimics the keys that fit the receptors on the type of cell they seek to infect. After attaching to the receptor, the virus either enters the cell or injects its genetic material into it. The virus uses the host cell's proteins and enzymes to replicate, or make more, viral genes and build new viral particles. These new viruses leave the cell and spread to a new host.

Defense System

The human body's immune system recognizes and destroys alien invaders such as viruses. Circulating in the blood, immune system cells come into contact with other cells. Each cell displays on its surface a sample of whatever material is being produced inside it.

ZIKA VIRUS EPIDEMIC

Zika virus is one virus that is spread through the bite of an infected insect, the mosquito. In 2015 and 2016, outbreaks of the virus occurred in the Americas. These cases spread to U.S. states through travel and spread quickly in Puerto Rico and the U.S. Virgin Islands. By 2017, the number of cases in the United States began to decline, and since 2018, there have been no reports of Zika virus in the United States. Still, this virus spread fear as people learned more about it.

Though mosquitoes are the main carrier of Zika, it can be passed from a pregnant woman to her fetus, or unborn baby. For most people, Zika causes mild symptoms such as fever, rash, headache, joint pain, eye redness, or muscle pain. In fact, many people are asymptomatic, or don't show symptoms, when infected. Why would an illness that isn't very severe spark fear? In cases of Zika passed from mother to fetus, severe birth defects of the brain, including **microcephaly**, can occur. Pregnant women and women of childbearing age were warned to be extra cautious during the height of the Zika virus outbreak. The fact that we have likely all had an unwanted mosquito bite in our lives makes the realities of viruses spread by them a little more worrisome.

Immune cells can distinguish between acceptable cell materials and foreign substances that don't belong. When immune cells encounter viruses or viral proteins, they destroy them.

The immune system's first line of defense is the skin. The outer skin has layers of dead cells. Viruses infect only living cells. Unless it is cut, skin presents an impenetrable barrier to viruses. Even "inner" skin, the cells lining the mucous membranes of the mouth, nose, and eyes, can block or destroy many germs.

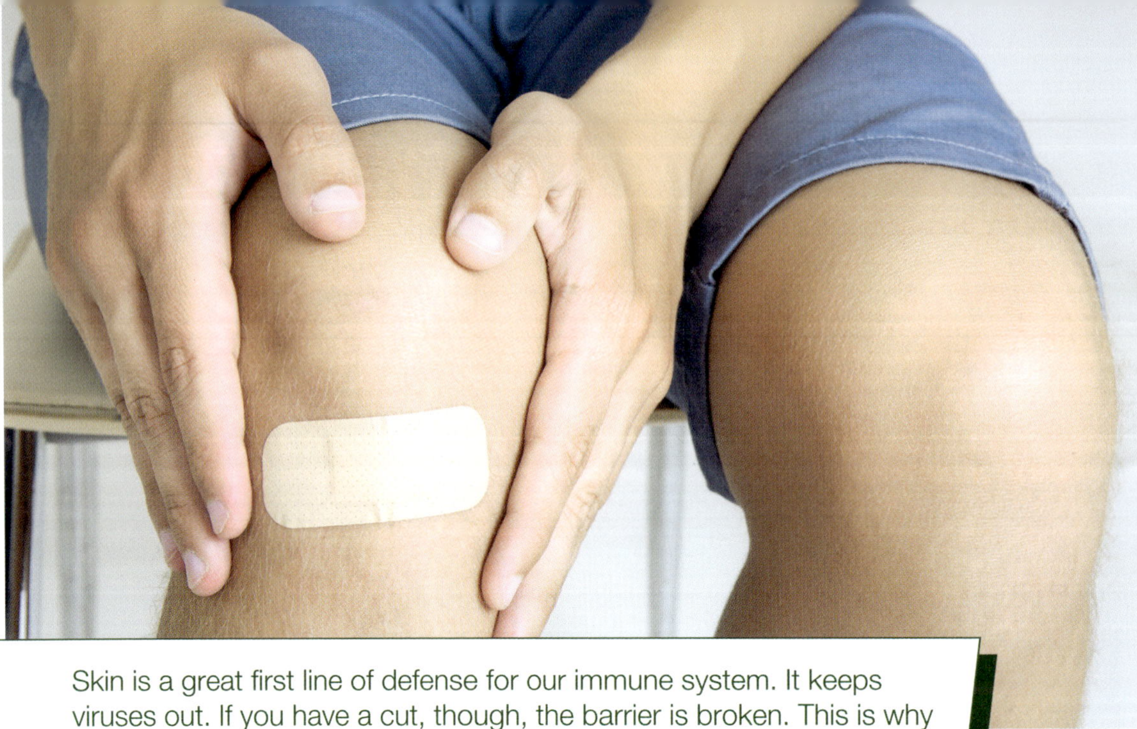

Skin is a great first line of defense for our immune system. It keeps viruses out. If you have a cut, though, the barrier is broken. This is why you should clean and cover wounds, creating an artificial barrier.

If a virus does get through and into the body, the next line of defense includes the leukocytes, or white blood cells, of which there are more than a dozen types. Cells such as phagocytes and **macrophages** work like the body's garbage collectors and consume viruses and debris from dead cells.

White blood cells known as B cells produce antibodies, which are chemicals that can bind to viruses and their antigens (the toxins they produce) and prevent their entry. These antibodies work together with about 20 different proteins produced in the liver that can kill viruses as part of the body's immune system. If these proteins fail to kill the viruses, they bind to them. Like warning flags, they signal infection to other immune cells that can kill the viruses.

Interferon is one such "alarm" protein. Infected cells usually produce huge amounts of RNA, which triggers interferon production in the cell. As its name suggests, interferon "interferes" with viral replication in infected cells. Interferon also binds to other cells and induces them to kill themselves to protect the body. Excess cell death, caused either by interferon or by viruses, activates other immune responses. Full-scale attack by the immune system causes **inflammation**. This results when some white blood cells release histamine, **dilating** blood vessels and bringing more blood and white blood cells to the site of infection.

Sometimes, a virus will invade the body and reproduce so quickly that it overwhelms the ability of antibodies and proteins to fight it. Then, the body brings out its big guns—the killer T cells. T cells have surface receptors that contain random segments of proteins, so they're extremely diverse. A T cell recognizes and destroys only those viruses whose proteins match its own.

Despite this impressive defense, the immune system sometimes has trouble fighting viral infections. Viruses use a variety of sneaky strategies to outwit the immune system or at least to hold it off long enough to allow them to reproduce and spread. They are also able to slightly mutate so the immune system's "memory" of how to destroy them isn't as effective.

WHAT DO YOU THINK?

1. How can we slow the spread of cold viruses?
2. How can learning about viruses help us fight diseases such as COVID-19?
3. Why do you think medical professionals often wear eye coverings when working with sick patients?

While colds aren't fun, as we get older our immune systems become accustomed to fighting the virus. Colds may make us feel under the weather, but the virus can be fended off quickly.

CHAPTER 2

WHAT DISEASES DO VIRUSES CAUSE?

It is undeniable that a virus has made every one of us sick at some point in our lives. There are more than 100 different cold viruses alone. In fact, because their immune systems are not yet strong, babies commonly have six to eight colds in their first year! Cold germs, often rhinoviruses, spread easily through droplets in the air or on surfaces. This is true of many viruses, but some viruses spread more slowly because the method of transmission is easier to avoid.

THE FLU

There are four types of influenza (flu) virus: A, B, C, and D. Human influenza A and B viruses cause what we know as the seasonal flu during the winter. Influenza A viruses are the only flu viruses that are known to cause global epidemics of the flu. Influenza C viruses generally cause mild illness in humans, and influenza D viruses mostly affect cattle; they are not known to cause illnesses in humans.

Influenza A is the deadliest and also the most **devious**. Influenza A targets cells of the respiratory system. Just hours after the initial infection, thousands of new viruses are created in the respiratory cells. This should trigger production of enormous quantities of interferon and activate the immune system. However, influenza A has a protein that partially disables interferon production in infected cells. This buys the flu time to reproduce and spread. Eventually, though, the death of so many respiratory cells triggers an immune response. The infected person develops antibodies against influenza A. However, the virus mutates so often that the immune system's defense against one strain is useless against mutant strains. This is why the flu is longer lasting and more serious than the common cold.

The flu vaccine is recommended for most people to help protect them from the seasonal flu. While the vaccine may not give you immunity against all strains of the flu that year, your immune system will have a head start if it has to fight the virus.

Flu transmission is similar to the transmission of the common cold. When an infected person talks, sneezes, or coughs, the virus travels through the air in droplets. You can inhale the droplets, or you can get the germs from touching an object, such as a cell phone or a doorknob, and then transferring the germs to your eyes, nose, or mouth. Once infected, a person may feel symptoms such as fever, chills, muscle aches, cough, congestion, runny or stuffy nose, headache, and fatigue. Because the flu mutates so often, a flu vaccine doesn't provide lifetime immunity; an annual vaccine provides a boost to your immune system when fighting the strains that may infect you.

Measles

Because of a very effective vaccination program, measles is rarely seen in the United States today, but it is still common in many parts of the world. Measles is a dangerous and very contagious virus that can infect the whole body because it has a surface protein that can connect to receptors on most body cells. New measles viruses bud from the infected cell and are carried in the blood to uninfected cells. Another reason that measles successfully infects the whole body is because it allows macrophages to kill it during its initial symptomless invasion of the lungs. As these viruses are killed, immune system cells carry samples of viral proteins to the lymph nodes, so the virus has actually infected these cells. The infected cells pass on the viral proteins to other immune cells in the lymph nodes. Infected immune cells carry the virus into the bloodstream and infect cells throughout the body. Epithelial cells, or cells that cover or line body parts, are especially targeted, causing the measles skin rash. Only killer T cells are able to finally destroy the virus.

The measles virus is transmitted in the same way as a cold or flu, but it can also be spread between mother and baby during pregnancy, labor, or breastfeeding. Because of the way it infects cells, symptoms don't occur until seven to fourteen days after exposure to the virus. Initial symptoms of a measles infection include high fever, cough, runny nose, and watery eyes; a skin rash appears three to five days after the first symptoms. There's only one strain of

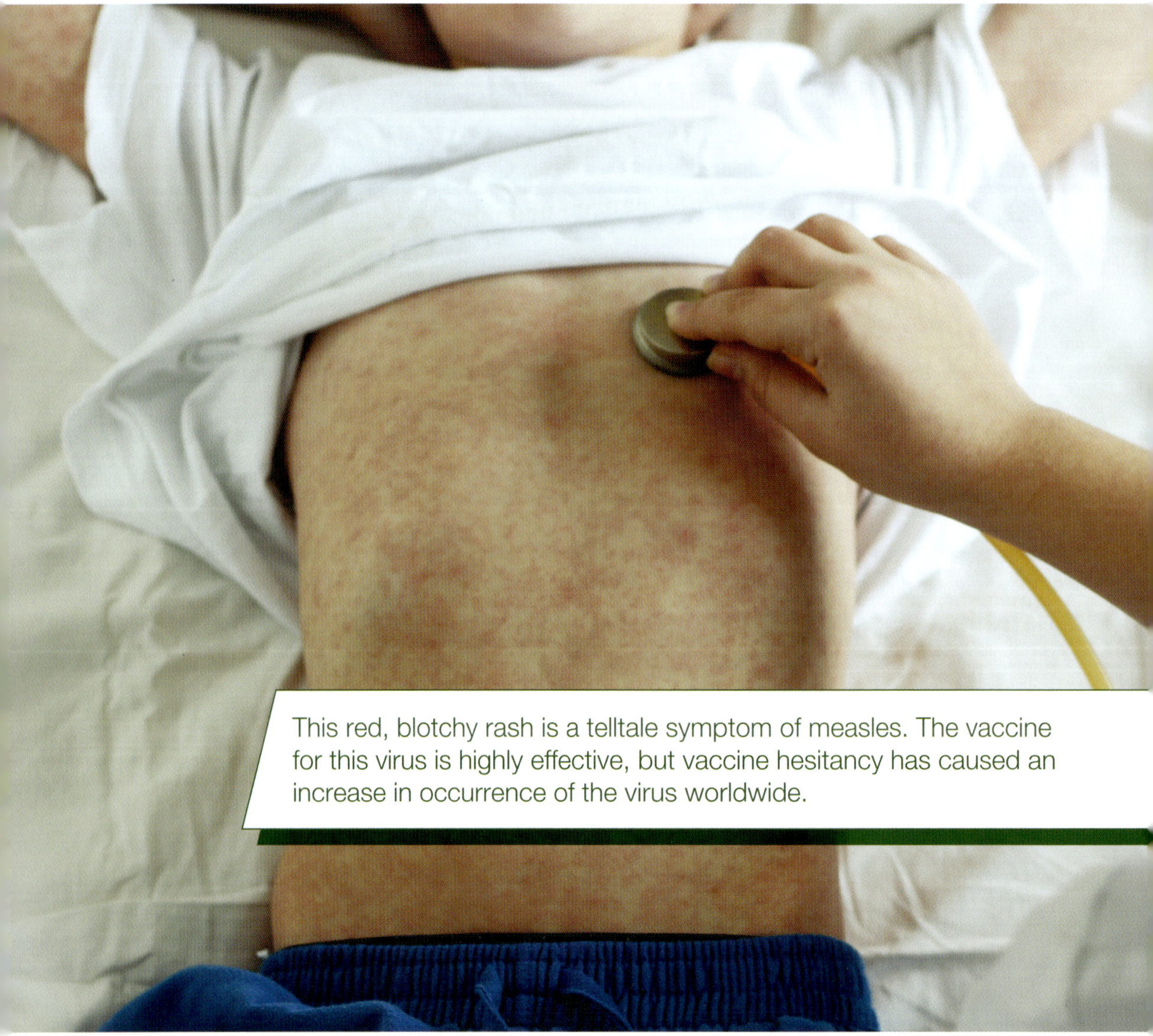

This red, blotchy rash is a telltale symptom of measles. The vaccine for this virus is highly effective, but vaccine hesitancy has caused an increase in occurrence of the virus worldwide.

measles, and it doesn't mutate. After infection, the body produces enough antibodies to prevent reinfection, and a person should have lifetime immunity. This is why vaccination for measles is so effective at preventing the disease.

Gastrointestinal (GI) Viruses

The gastrointestinal (GI) tract runs all the way through the body and includes the organs in the digestive system. When you get a GI virus, it affects something along that tract, often the intestines, making you sick. **Enteric adenoviruses** infect the intestines. They are spread when virus-contaminated water, food, or feces is ingested, and they are most prevalent where unsanitary conditions exist. Millions of children die every year from adenovirus-induced diarrhea.

Enteric adenoviruses have stronger protein coatings that enable them to withstand acids in the digestive tract as they head toward the intestines. These acids eat partway through the coating, and the virus's genetic material is free to infect cells. In two days, one infected cell can produce 100,000 adenoviruses.

Adenovirus replication might make it vulnerable to immune attack, but the virus is prepared. An adenovirus contains proteins that prevent the death of infected and neighboring cells so cell death does not trigger the immune system. Adenovirus proteins also prevent the infected cell from displaying viral material on its surface, so killer T cells are not alerted to the infection. Another viral protein prevents attack by natural killer cells—another kind of immune cell. Only after the virus has spread throughout the intestines are these immune cells finally able to combat it.

GI viruses are not pleasant to deal with. A big concern with them is dehydration, so keeping down fluids is crucial. While these viruses are often called the "stomach flu," influenza does not cause their symptoms.

Rotavirus and norovirus are other viral GI diseases. They are spread in the same way as enteric adenovirus. A vaccine is available for rotavirus to prevent severe infection and reduce the likelihood of any rotavirus infection in children.

Hepatitis

The hepatitis A virus is also spread by contaminated food, water, and waste. Like the adenovirus and other GI viruses, it enters the body through the mouth. The single existing strain of hepatitis A targets liver cells. The well-armored, acid-resistant virus travels the digestive tract to the intestines. Here the virus infects cells and reproduces much like a rhinovirus—with one important difference. Hepatitis A rarely kills infected cells, unlike a cold virus.

In the intestines, hepatitis A produces a limited infection that is easily neutralized by the immune system's B cells, but the B cells carry it from the intestines to the liver for disposal. A weak intestinal virus then becomes a powerful disease agent. Infected liver cells make countless copies of hepatitis A's single-stranded RNA before an immune response in the liver finally finishes them off. Meanwhile, the new viruses move from the liver to the bile ducts, back into the intestines, then out of the body with feces. The virus spreads so effectively because it remains viable for weeks in dried feces.

Hepatitis B also infects liver cells. It is mostly passed from mother to child in the womb or in breast milk. It can also be spread by direct blood-to-blood contact. Hepatitis B can cause either acute or chronic infection. An acute infection is eventually **eradicated** when killer T cells destroy infected liver cells. Though the viral infection is gone, lifelong liver damage may result. About 90 percent of infants born with the virus live with a chronic, symptomless hepatitis B infection. Infected females will pass hepatitis B on to their children.

Hepatitis C causes a chronic infection. It, too, attacks the liver. Hepatitis C was first identified in 1989, so little is known about it, yet it currently affects about 170 million people worldwide. The virus binds to macrophages. It also attaches to **lipoproteins** in the blood. Because every body cell needs lipoproteins, all cells have receptors for it, but the virus prefers to bind to liver cells. Infected liver cells produce up to a trillion viruses daily!

The error rate in copying hepatitis C's genes is very large. Its constant mutations drive the immune system crazy. After the initial infection, antibodies and killer T cells recognize and conquer the virus. Just when the enemy seems to be wiped out, one or more mutant strains of hepatitis C virus emerge and attack. The immune system must start from scratch to fight them. This cat-and-mouse game occurs in six-week cycles. The virus is careful not to mutate too rapidly and risk killing its host. It also cannot mutate too slowly and risk being demolished by the immune system. Slow and steady mutation maintains an active and chronic infection.

Hepatitis C is transmitted from mother to child or through blood-to-blood contact. It is spread to children mostly during childbirth. Intravenous drug users who share needles may transmit the infection through blood, as may blood transfusions. In most cases, people with chronic hepatitis C infections suffer no symptoms for decades. Eventually, continuous cycles of infection cause **cirrhosis** of the liver, which can be fatal.

Hepatitis A and B both have vaccines to help prevent the diseases. As of now, a vaccine is not available for hepatitis C.

Herpes

There are several types of herpes virus. All produce lifelong, chronic infection. Herpes viruses are transmitted by physical contact and are often transmitted sexually.

Herpes simplex virus (HSV) produces a chronic infection by keeping a low profile in the body after initial infection. HSV invades epithelial cells around the skin and mucous membranes. By the time the epithelial infection is defeated, the virus has created an escape

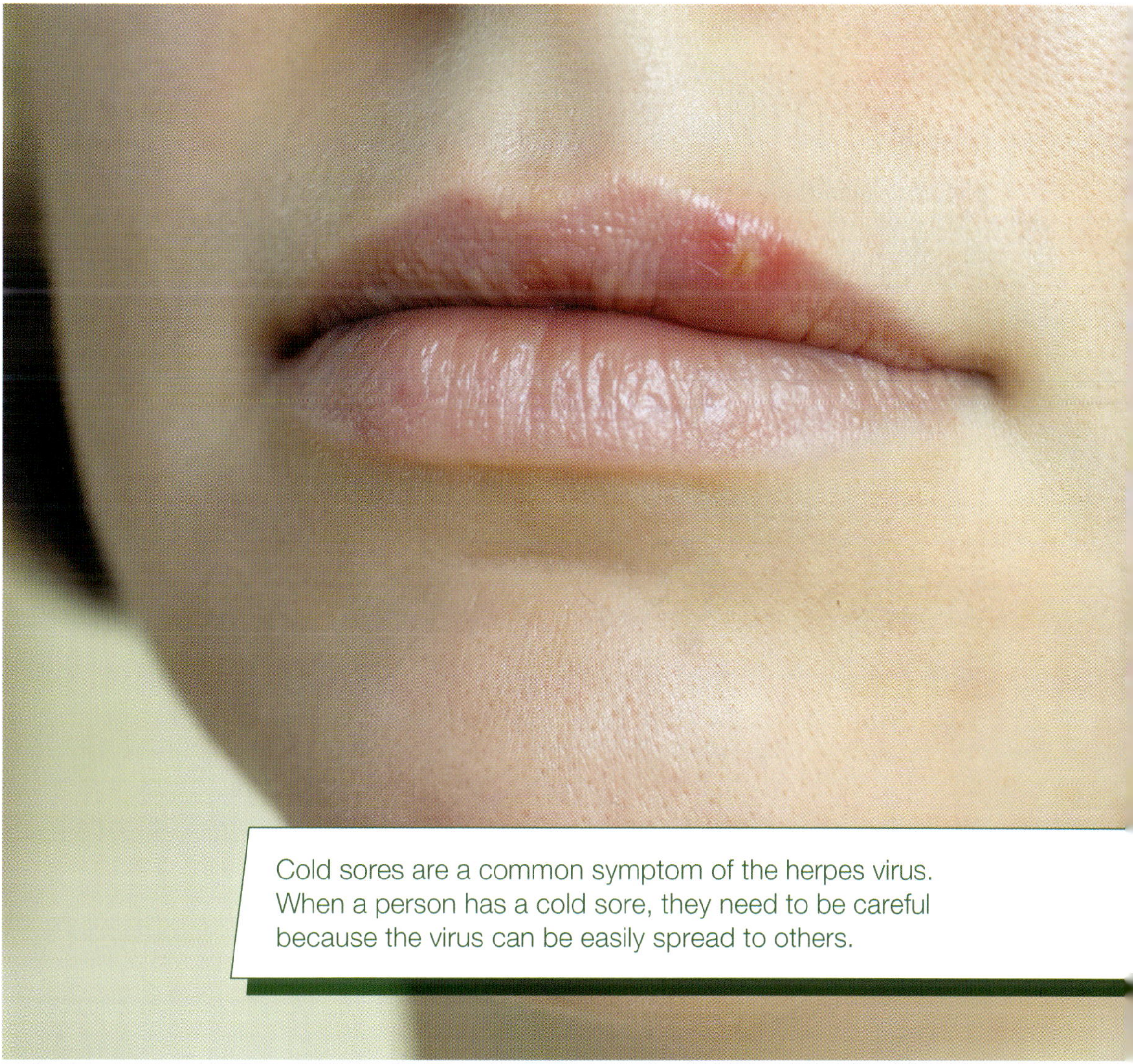

Cold sores are a common symptom of the herpes virus. When a person has a cold sore, they need to be careful because the virus can be easily spread to others.

route: a cold sore. Cold sores contain thousands of viruses, ready to spread to new hosts through direct contact or through saliva.

Infection of epithelial cells is only half the HSV story. A virus spread through physical contact must remain in the body to be transmitted to others. After leaving the epithelial cells, some HSV migrates to nearby sensory nerve cells. HSV cannot reproduce in nerve cells, but it can hide in them. Once HSV is inside nerve cells, the immune system is unaware of it. This hidden infection lasts a lifetime. Occasionally, some HSV awakens, leaves the nerve cells, and reinfects epithelial cells, causing a painful skin disease.

Chickenpox

Chickenpox is a common childhood disease caused by the herpes varicella-zoster virus (VZV). The first time you get VZV, it always causes chickenpox. Chickenpox is spread by contact with its virus-filled skin blisters. B cells destroy chickenpox and produce antibodies to ensure you never get it again. However, like HSV, VZV hides in nerve cells. VZV may remain dormant in nerve cells for decades or, if you're lucky, forever, but sometimes, VZV reawakens. When it does, it always shows up as shingles, a painful skin disorder. Shingles blisters are full of VZV, and contact with them spreads the virus. The virus that causes chickenpox does not mutate, so a vaccine is an effective way to gain immunity to VZV without having an active infection. In older adults, a shingles vaccine can prepare the immune system in the case VZV reawakens.

HPV

One virus sometimes confused with herpes is the human papillomavirus (HPV), probably because it produces skin warts. Each of the hundred or so HPVs specializes in infecting basal cells (in the innermost part of the skin) in a particular part of the body. At some stage, HPV replicates wildly in basal cells, eventually pushing masses of infected cells to the skin surface, producing a wart. Physical contact spreads the virus to a new host.

Skin cells are always being replaced, and thus basal cells are always reproducing. This makes them a great candidate for targeting by viruses, producing chronic infections. HPV also attacks the immune system by creating proteins that prevent adjacent cells from dying. These characteristics of HPV make it stick around for good. While killer T cells take care of some HPV cells, sleeper viruses hiding out in basal cells lie in wait to infect the host again. Without treatment, sometimes HPV can cause cancer.

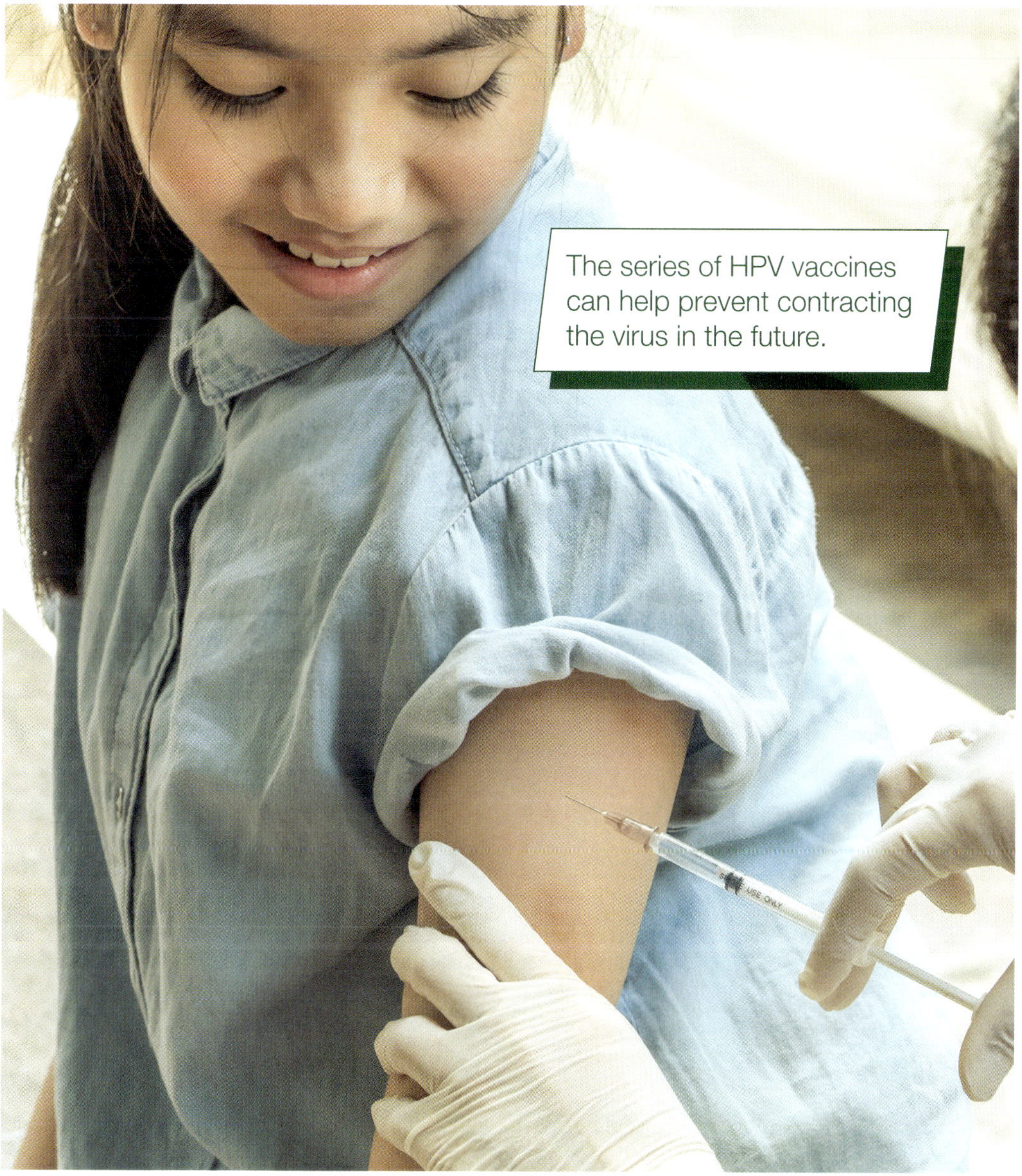

The series of HPV vaccines can help prevent contracting the virus in the future.

CORONAVIRUSES

Coronaviruses enter through the nose, mouth, or eyes. The outer spike protein latches onto the receptors of the cells in our respiratory tract. Once the cells are infected, they may produce and release millions of copies of the virus. Coronaviruses can cause mild cold-like symptoms or severe respiratory symptoms. COVID-19 is the first of this class of viruses to have an approved vaccine. Booster doses, as with the flu and other viruses that often mutate, seem to provide increased immune protection.

Covering the nose and mouth with a mask can be an effective method to fight against the spread of coronaviruses. If both the infected host and the potential new host have this extra barrier on their airways, the spread of the virus will be slowed.

EBOLA OUTBREAK

From 2014 to 2016, there was an outbreak of a virus called Ebola in the West African countries of Guinea, Liberia, and Sierra Leone. Ebola is a hemorrhagic virus, meaning it causes severe bleeding at a later stage in the infection. Because of its fearsome symptoms, this outbreak was noticed around the world. The 2014 outbreak is believed to have been spread by bats in a rural area of West Africa. It spread to more populated cities before it was identified as Ebola. While scientists had seen strains of the virus before, it had never spread out of isolated rural areas. This outbreak eventually spread to seven other countries including Italy, Mali, Nigeria, Senegal, Spain, the United Kingdom, and the United States. By the time the outbreak ended, more than 28,600 cases and 11,325 deaths were recorded, mostly in West Africa.

Viral hemorrhagic fevers (VHFs) are not new. They include not only Ebola, but Marburg, Lassa fever, and yellow fever too. These viruses all affect many organs and damage blood vessels. While risk is low when there isn't an outbreak, some of these VHFs have no effective treatment, raising concern that they could be used in germ warfare.

WHAT DO YOU THINK?

1. Have you ever had one of the viruses described in this chapter? If so, how did you feel, and how did you treat it?
2. Why do you think stomach viruses are often called the "stomach flu" if influenza does not cause them?
3. How does vaccine hesitancy affect how common a virus such as measles is?

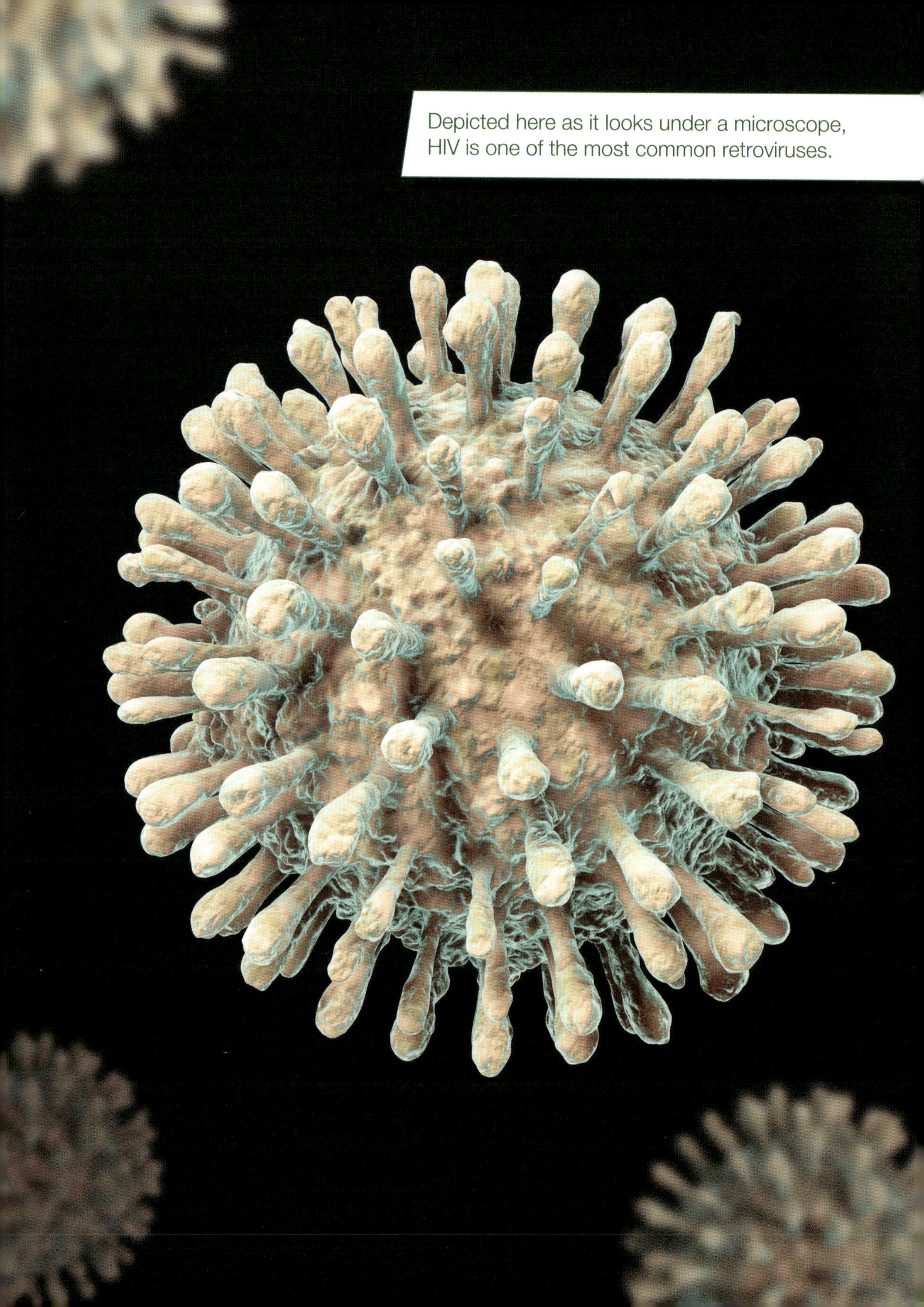

Depicted here as it looks under a microscope, HIV is one of the most common retroviruses.

CHAPTER 3

WHAT ARE RETROVIRUSES?

Retroviruses are a unique group of RNA viruses. When one infects a cell, it makes a copy of itself that is inserted in the host cell's DNA. These viruses are especially dangerous because they don't attract the attention of our immune systems. When the host cell reproduces normally, the retrovirus also reproduces.

HTLV-1

HTLV-1 (human T-lymphotropic virus, type 1) was the first retrovirus discovered, in 1980. HTLV-1 attaches to and infects helper T cells via an unknown receptor on the cell surface. It then replicates in helper T cells. A viral enzyme called integrase cuts the cell's DNA and inserts the viral genetic material into the cell's genes. Every time the infected helper T cell reproduces, the new cells contain the virus's genes. Replication of HTLV-1 is thus rather slow, depending as it does on cell division. HTLV-1 doesn't kill the infected cells it relies on to reproduce. Most of the time, HTLV-1 lies low. Infected people carry it for life, but about 95 percent never suffer from an HTLV1-induced disease.

Decades after infection, about 5 percent of infected people will develop cancer. HTLV-1 is associated with adult T-cell leukemia. Causing a disease that kills its host (along with the virus) is an unintended result of infection. Scientists believe leukemia arises because the viral genetic material eventually causes mutations in the helper T cell's own genes. HTLV-1 is spread through blood, so intravenous drug users may transmit it. It can also be spread through bodily fluids during sexual activity. Women with HTLV-1 in their blood may pass it to infants through breast milk.

HIV/AIDS

HIV (human immunodeficiency virus), another retrovirus, was first identified in 1983. It was soon shown to cause AIDS (acquired immunodeficiency syndrome), a devastating and deadly condition that destroys the immune system.

HIV infects immune system cells with certain surface receptors. Its primary targets are helper T cells and macrophages. HIV's RNA enters the host cell's genes in typical retrovirus fashion. However, HIV also has a protein that boosts its infection rate. When an infected cell begins proliferating, this protein induces the cell to produce a thousand times more HIV genes than cell genes. The new viruses, many of them mutants, bud from the cell, enter the blood, and seek more cells to infect.

Initially, HIV infects macrophages and other cells, but it doesn't kill them. At this early stage, there are enough helper T cells to activate killer T cells, which control the HIV infection. Initial infection usually causes flulike symptoms, which disappear in a few weeks. Then, HIV begins a period of latency.

Though the infection seems to be under control during latency, wave after wave of macrophages and other cells become infected with HIV. The immune system produces helper T cells, which mobilize killer T cells to fight the virus. This battle against HIV is continuous and ferocious. Yet the person infected with HIV feels perfectly healthy. There are no outward signs of infection, though HIV is present in blood and other body fluids. It is during latency that HIV is most often spread by unaware carriers.

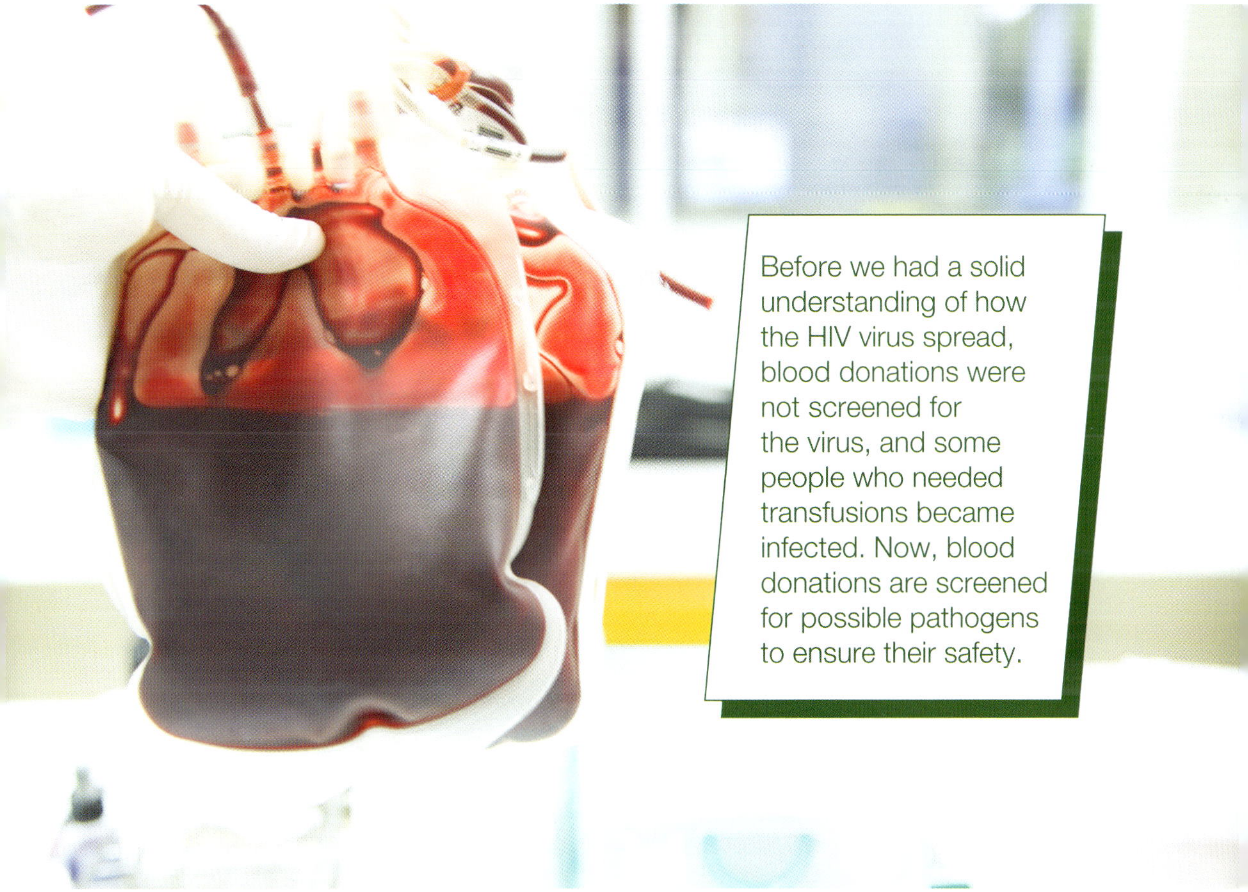

Before we had a solid understanding of how the HIV virus spread, blood donations were not screened for the virus, and some people who needed transfusions became infected. Now, blood donations are screened for possible pathogens to ensure their safety.

HIV completely disrupts the immune system and turns it against itself. At some point during the long latency, HIV mutates in such a way that infected cells are able to pass the virus on to helper T cells in the lymph nodes. HIV kills the helper T cells it infects. Helper T cells are crucial to the immune system. Without them, B cells and killer T cells are not generated.

HIV IN T CELLS

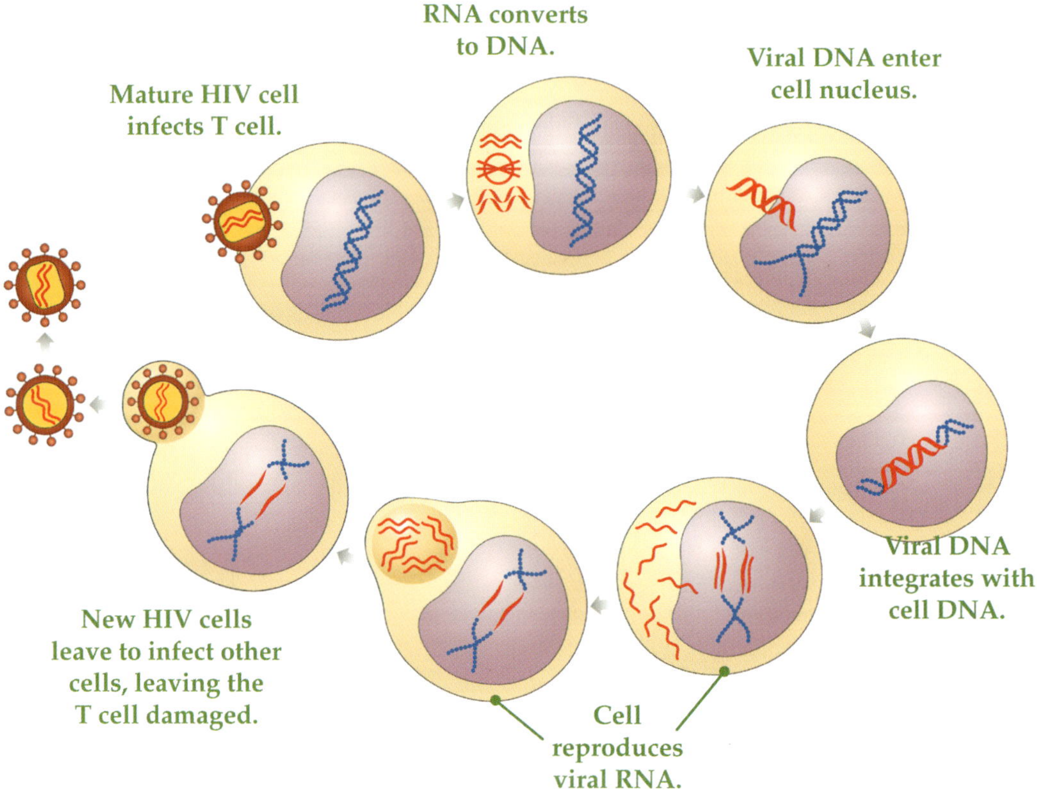

This diagram shows how HIV infects helper T cells and is able to destroy them.

In the lymph nodes, HIV infects millions and then billions of helper T cells. The infected cells proliferate, each producing thousands of viruses, and then are killed. The lymph nodes become huge reservoirs, or holding spaces, for the virus. They turn into HIV factories where 100 billion new viruses are produced every day!

The desperate immune system cranks out billions of new helper T cells a day. However, they, too, quickly become infected with mutant HIV. The more helper T cells the body produces, the worse the infection becomes. Instead of fighting the infection, these desperately needed immune system cells are themselves infected, produce more HIV, and are then killed by it. The result is a relentless downward spiral in which the supply of helper T cells dwindles to almost nothing and mutant HIV overruns the immune system.

A microliter of healthy human blood contains about 1,200 T cells. A microliter of blood from a person completely overrun by HIV contains only 200 T cells. With so few helper T cells, the

HIV and AIDS severely weaken the immune system, and infections that wouldn't affect a healthy person can make an infected individual very sick. Today, as research has advanced, there are medications to prevent HIV from developing into full-blown AIDS and keep people with the virus healthy for a very long time.

HIV CRISIS

In the 1980s, the outbreak of HIV and AIDS swept across the world. Although HIV in humans existed decades earlier, and even around 10 years prior in the United States, the 1980s brought the virus to public attention. In 1981, the Centers for Disease Control and Prevention (CDC) published a report about five gay men infected with a pneumonia that was normally harmless. It was concerning because the men seemed healthy, but the CDC noted that this disease almost never affects those with healthy immune systems. The following year, more cases of this "immune system disorder" were noticed. Because many of the affected people were gay men, it was initially mistaken for a disease that was related to their sexuality. Even after the CDC discovered how the disease was transmitted, the public still considered it a "gay disease" for many years.

This stigma hurt an already marginalized group. On top of that, these men feared a disease that their friends and loved ones were dying from. Even today, public health outreach to prevent the spread of HIV must work to bypass the stigma around the disease to reach populations that benefit from education on the virus.

Because people thought AIDS only affected gay men, the epidemic did not initially get the research or attention it needed. Protests like this helped raise awareness and speed up the process of finding effective treatment.

immune system is essentially destroyed. The infected person now has AIDS. In a person with AIDS, up to 2 billion immune system cells are killed in the body every day.

Opportunistic infections—infections that healthy immune systems easily defeat—can often overwhelm AIDS sufferers. In fact, these are often the direct cause of death for those who catch HIV. One of the first opportunistic infections to plague AIDS patients is herpes virus 8, the cause of a type of skin cancer called Kaposi's sarcoma.

The body can be overcome by a host of different fungal, bacterial, and viral infections, many which are otherwise rare for healthy individuals. Common ailments include untreatable strains of pneumonia or tuberculosis. Brain infections causing memory loss, tremors, epilepsy, and even psychosis can occur, as well as bacterial infections that bring on neurological disorders. In general, HIV enables a whole host of horrific diseases and conditions.

WHAT DO YOU THINK?

1. Why are retroviruses so hard for the body to defend against?
2. Can you think of any other diseases or medical conditions that have a stigma around them, such as the one that surrounded HIV and AIDS in the 1980s? How can we stop these stigmas?
3. Why do you think infections that healthy immune systems easily beat are called opportunistic?

Bats are one of the animals known to spread diseases. Some strains of coronaviruses and Ebola are examples of viruses passed from bats to humans.

HOW CAN WE PREPARE FOR NEW VIRUSES?

CHAPTER 4

Viruses don't affect only people. All over the world, known and unknown viruses specific to animals exist. Sometimes these diseases or strains can be transmitted to humans; they are known as **zoonotic** diseases. This includes zoonotic influenza such as the H1N1 strain commonly known as the swine flu, West Nile virus, and rabies. It also includes emerging coronaviruses including the virus responsible for the COVID-19 pandemic. As viruses we have not previously dealt with in humans begin to infect us, science and medicine must move quickly to understand and treat these emerging diseases.

VACCINATIONS

A vaccine is a preparation intended to be harmless to the recipient but sufficiently potent to initiate an immune response when put into the body. In the course of fighting the introduced substance, the immune system produces antibodies that stay in the body and safeguard against future infection.

Some noninfectious vaccines are made from dead viruses. The defunct viruses generate memory immune cells but generally don't cause infection. Some polio vaccines are made this way. Another strategy is to make viruses out of pieces of viral proteins or viral

DNA. These vaccines stimulate the immune system to produce antibodies. Because the vaccine contains incomplete parts of viruses, an infection cannot occur. This type of vaccine is effective against hepatitis B.

Attenuated or weakened viruses are grown in the tissues of nonhuman animals. When injected into humans as a vaccine, the weakened virus is unable to cause infection, but it does induce antibody production. Attenuated vaccines immunize against mumps, measles, and rubella (German measles), and have the advantage of producing lifelong immunity, something that noninfectious vaccines cannot guarantee. Finally, there are new vaccines whose DNA induces production of both memory B cells and killer T cells. The vaccine is made from DNA that codes for only a few viral proteins, so it cannot cause infection.

In the case of COVID-19, messenger RNA (mRNA) vaccines have proven effective. These vaccines tell the cells to create what is called a spike protein. The spike protein is also found on the surface of the COVID-19 virus. After the mRNA does its job, it is broken down by the cells, but the spike protein is displayed on their surface. This triggers an immune response and prepares the body so if it were to be infected with actual COVID-19, it would know how to fight it.

Treatments

Sometimes vaccines are used to treat, not prevent, viral infection. The rabies vaccine is an example. Rabies reproduces slowly in the body and usually takes a rather long time to reach its destination in the brain. A vaccine administered after infection usually gives the immune system enough time to mobilize and destroy the infection.

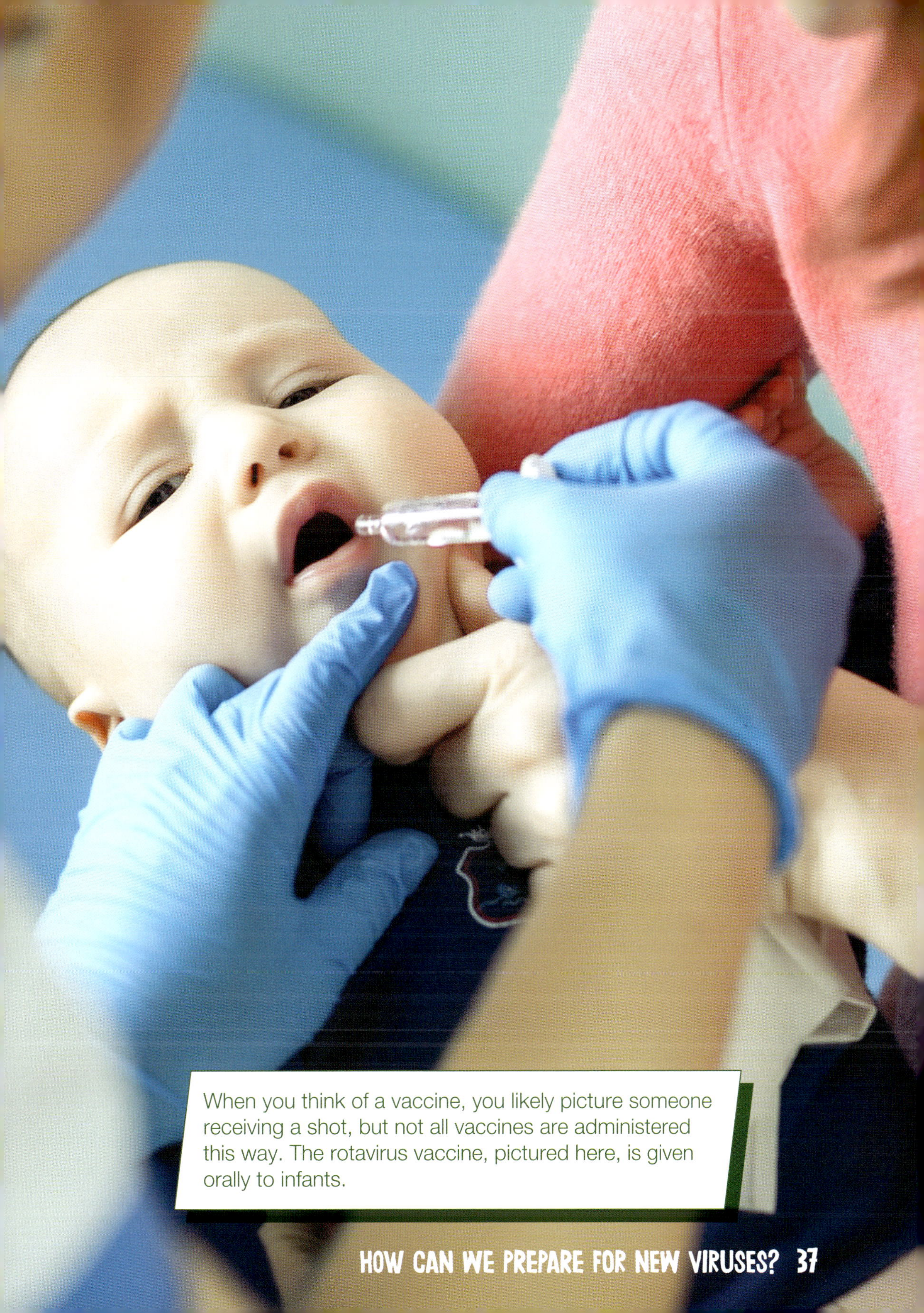

When you think of a vaccine, you likely picture someone receiving a shot, but not all vaccines are administered this way. The rotavirus vaccine, pictured here, is given orally to infants.

mRNA VACCINE

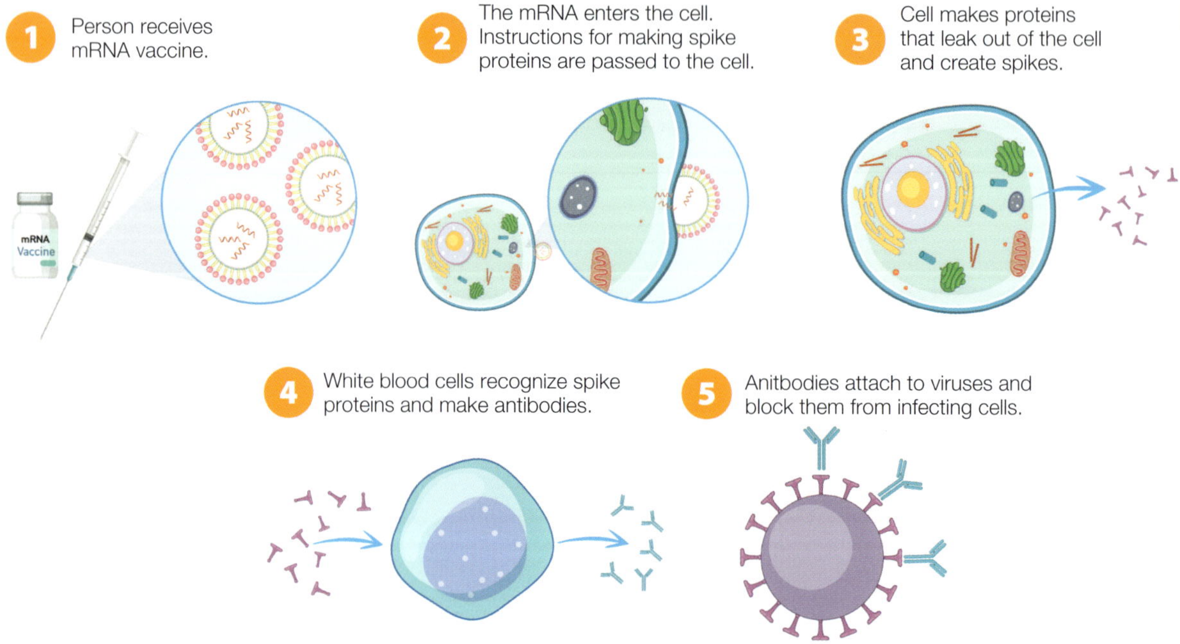

This is how mRNA vaccines work. These kinds of vaccines do not make a person sick with the virus or cause them to become contagious.

Aside from vaccines, antiviral drugs aim to disrupt viruses during one particular stage of infection: during entry, uncoating, gene replication, or exit from a cell. To date, no drug can disrupt a virus's entry into a cell.

One new drug can disrupt the uncoating of the influenza A virus. The drug interferes with a viral protein that "unzips" the virus's coat, so viral genes cannot be released into the cell. Though promising, the drug cannot counter influenza A's rapid mutation rate, which alters the targeted viral protein.

AZT, a drug used to treat HIV, interferes with the replication of the retrovirus. Enzymes in the cell convert AZT into a protein that attaches to viral DNA, preventing the DNA from assembling and stopping replication.

A nocturnal animal such as a raccoon that acts strangely during the day might be infected with the rabies virus. While public health measures are taken in most places to try to prevent rabies from occurring in wild animals, a vaccine can help if the disease is spread from animal to human.

Viruses are common threats to our health today, and there will likely be emerging viruses in the future that we have not yet researched. Even though viruses are prevalent, so are the scientists and researchers striving to learn new information about them. Every advance in medicine helps us prepare to treat and fight viruses more effectively as we continue our war against germs.

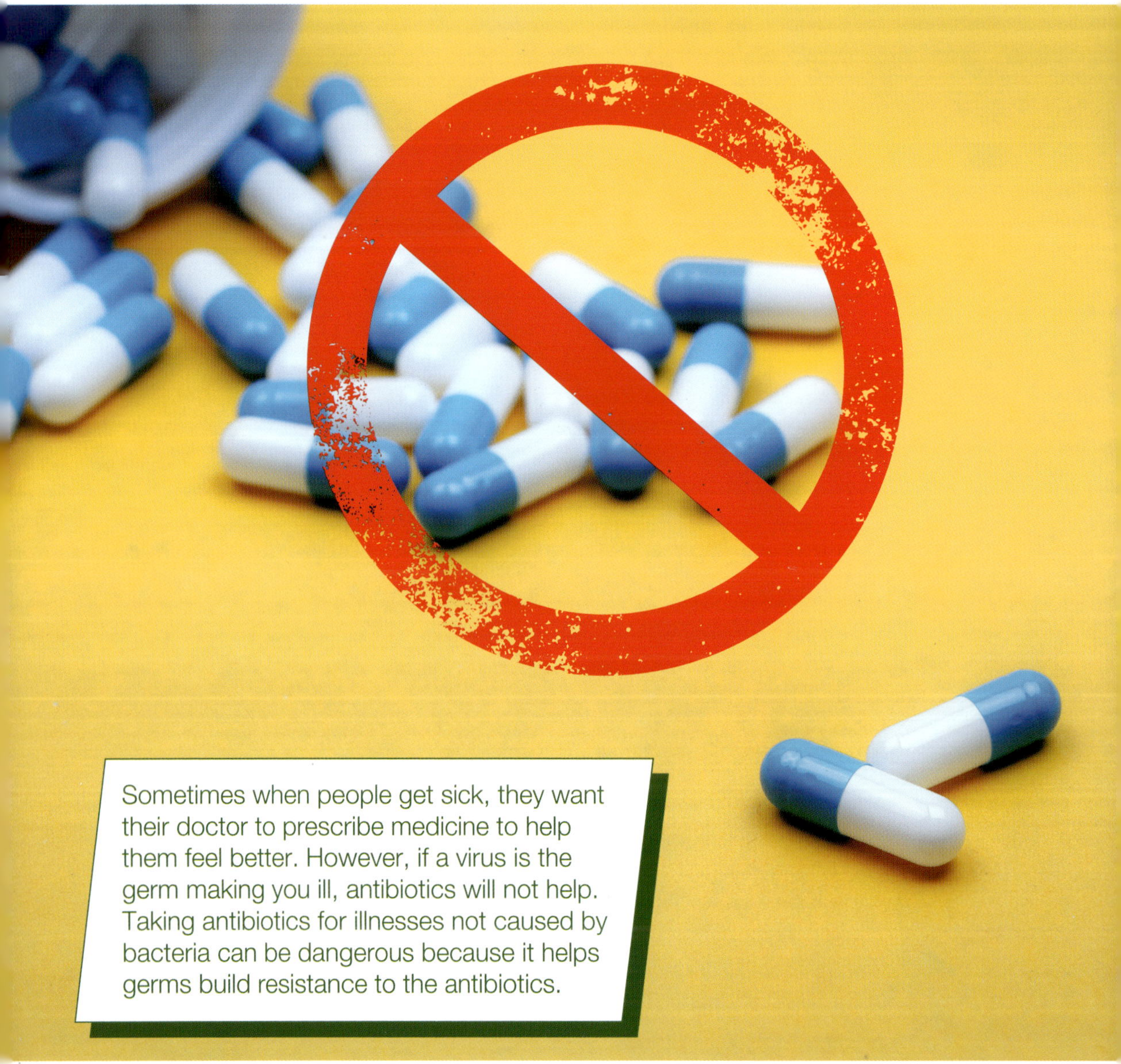

Sometimes when people get sick, they want their doctor to prescribe medicine to help them feel better. However, if a virus is the germ making you ill, antibiotics will not help. Taking antibiotics for illnesses not caused by bacteria can be dangerous because it helps germs build resistance to the antibiotics.

ERADICATED DISEASE

Thanks to vaccines, smallpox is a viral disease that has been eradicated, or eliminated worldwide. After causing millions of deaths throughout history, smallpox was declared eradicated by the World Health Organization (WHO) in 1980.

In 1967, the WHO launched a program called the Intensified Eradication Program, renewing the efforts of a previously underfunded plan to rid the world of smallpox. This helped provide higher quality vaccines and resources to the continents that needed them. By 1971, smallpox was eliminated from South America. It was soon followed by Asia in 1975 and Africa in 1977, largely a result of the efforts of the eradication program. (The elimination of smallpox in North America and Europe had occurred in the 1950s, and Australia never had widespread cases of the virus.) After a few years of monitoring for cases, smallpox was officially declared eradicated in one of the biggest public health victories of the modern era. Samples of variola virus, which causes smallpox, do still exist in laboratory stocks and have been studied under WHO supervision.

WHAT DO YOU THINK?

1. As humans occupy more of the planet, why do you think new viruses are making us ill?
2. Why do you think some people might be hesitant to receive vaccines? How would you respond to this hesitancy?
3. Why do you think it is important to continue to research viruses we already successfully treat?

GLOSSARY

cirrhosis: A chronic disease of the liver, typically a result of alcoholism or hepatitis.

deoxyribonucleic acid: The hereditary material found in cells.

devious: Skillfully using underhanded tactics to achieve goals.

dilate: To make or become wider, larger, or more open.

enteric adenovirus: An often fatal intestinal virus that causes diarrhea.

eradicated: Destroyed completely.

host: An organism that is invaded by and whose life functions support a virus or other parasite.

inflammation: A bodily response to injury or infection in which heat, redness, and swelling are often present.

interferon: A signaling or alarm protein that interferes with viral replication in infected cells.

lipoprotein: A protein that combines with and transports fat.

macrophage: One of the cells in the human immune systems that engulfs foreign particles or cells, acting as a scavenger or "garbage collector" within the body.

microcephaly: A condition characterized by abnormal smallness of the head associated with incomplete brain development.

pandemic: A huge outbreak of infection, often spanning multiple continents or the whole world.

ribonucleic acid: A substance found mainly in the cytoplasm that carries out DNA's instructions for making vital cell proteins.

zoonotic: Referring to a disease that can be transmitted from animals to humans.

FIND OUT MORE

BOOKS

Hansen, Grace. *The COVID-19 Virus*. Minneapolis, MN: ABDO Publishing, 2021.

Macgregor, Eloise. *Be a Virus Warrior! A Kid's Guide to Keeping Safe.* New York, NY: PowerKids Press, 2020.

Martynoga, Ben. *The Virus*. Oxford, UK: David Fickling Books, 2020.

WEBSITES

Boston Children's Hospital
childrenshospital.org/covid19
This site has easy-to-understand graphics and information about how the COVID-19 virus affects children and teens.

Nemours KidsHealth: "A Kid's Guide to Shots"
kidshealth.org/en/kids/guide-shots.html
This site provides health information geared toward kids, teens, and parents and specifically has easy-to-understand information about vaccinations.

The Well Project
thewellproject.org/hiv-information/talking-your-children-about-hiv-hiv-awareness-children
This public health outreach organization has resources to help parents talk to their children about HIV.

ORGANIZATIONS

Centers for Disease Control and Prevention (CDC)
1600 Clifton Road
Atlanta, GA 30329
www.cdc.gov
The Centers for Disease Control and Prevention (CDC) is the primary U.S. government agency in charge of tracking, treating, and preventing public health threats, including infectious diseases caused by viruses.

Doctors Without Borders
40 Rector Street, 16th floor
New York, NY 10006
www.doctorswithoutborders.org
Doctors Without Borders (founded originally by French doctors in 1970 as Médecins Sans Frontières) is an international humanitarian organization dedicated to providing medical aid to civilians in war zones and citizens of developing nations facing disease.

National Institutes of Health (NIH)
9000 Rockville Pike
Bethesda, MD 20892
Email: NIHinfo@od.nih.gov
www.nih.gov
The National Institutes of Health (NIH) is a research facility in the Washington, D.C., area and the primary agency of the U.S. government in charge of biomedical and health-related research.

Publisher's note to educators and parents: Our editors have carefully reviewed these websites to ensure that they are suitable for students. Many websites change frequently, however, and we cannot guarantee that a site's future contents will continue to meet our high standards of quality and educational value. Be advised that students should be closely supervised whenever they access the internet.

INDEX

About the Author

Kathryn Kroe has a master's degree in public health from the University at Buffalo and a bachelor's degree in education from SUNY Buffalo State College. She is passionate about spreading accurate information and helping young people understand issues pertaining to their health and the health of those around them. She currently lives in Lockport, New York, with her husband and two toddlers. She enjoys walking with her family, playing with her Australian shepherd, Zoey, and traveling to see new places.